AN
EASY-READ
FACT
BOOK

Farm Animals

Angela Hart

Franklin Watts
London New York Toronto Sydney

© 1982 Franklin Watts Ltd

First published in Great Britain
  1982 by
Franklin Watts Ltd
8 Cork Street
London W1

First published in the USA by
Franklin Watts Inc.
387 Park Avenue South
New York
N.Y. 10016

UK ISBN: 0 85166 959 X
US ISBN: 0-531-04447-5
Library of Congress Catalog Card
  Number: 82-50065

Printed in Great Britain by
  Cambus Litho, East Kilbride

Photographs supplied by
Australian Information Service
ISA Poultry Services Ltd
David Jefferis
Milk Marketing Board

Illustrated by
Christopher Forsey
Hayward Art Group
N. E. Middleton Ltd

Designed and produced by
David Jefferis

Technical consultant
Tony Jefferis, Manager of
  Knighton Wood Farm

AN
EASY-READ
FACT
BOOK

Farm Animals

Contents

Animals on the farm

▽ This scene shows French farm life 500 years ago. Oxen drag a plow through the soil. The plow breaks up the surface so that seeds can be sown. Geese supply eggs and meat, while goat's supply meat, milk and cheese.

About 10,000 years ago the first farmers were growing crops in the warm climate of the Middle East. It is thought that about this time, too, the first animals were tamed for use on the farm. It was better to have a supply of fresh meat close to hand than relying completely on hunting. If game was scarce for some reason, then a tribe could go hungry.

Farm animals were useful for other things besides their meat. Milk and

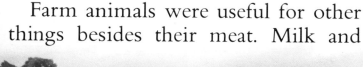

4

◁ The powerful diesel tractor has replaced oxen and horses on modern farms. Machines like this can pull anything from plows to heavily laden grain trailers.

eggs were good to eat. The wool of sheep and goats could be woven to make cloth. Oxen could be harnessed to pull heavy carts and drag plows through rocky soil, jobs that were previously done by the farmers.

Ancestors of the animals

△ Here you see some of the ancestors of today's farm animals. Wild geese and ducks fly through the air. Below them stands an aurochs, the ancestor of most cattle breeds. Pigs are descended from the wild boar, and chickens from the jungle fowl of south-east Asia. Wild sheep lived in mountain areas.

Long ago, before there were farmers, the ancestors of today's farm animals were wild creatures. Many of them looked very different from their modern descendants. As you can see in the picture above, a wild boar does not look much like a pig.

The farm animals we have today are mostly the result of careful breeding. Beef cattle have been raised to provide bigger joints of better quality meat.

Sheep grow heavier and finer fleeces. Hens lay more eggs. And often, during the course of breeding, the size, shape and color of the animals have changed.

All sorts of animals are used by people around the world. In the deserts of the Middle East, camels are still used as beasts of burden, as are water buffalo in India and Asia. In Scandinavia reindeer steak is a popular food.

△ The range of domestic animals is very wide. Here you see a camel, a water buffalo and a reindeer. They are useful to people in different parts of the world.

Cattle

Cattle are kept for two main reasons, for their meat and for their milk.

Beef cattle are very bulky. The best breeds, such as Charolais and Herefords, have big hindquarters which is where the tastiest cuts of meat come from. Dairy cattle, such as Holsteins and Ayrshires, are those raised mainly for their milk. Each cow has a big udder with four teats. It is from these that they are milked twice a day, morning and evening.

Apart from meat and milk, cattle provide lots of other useful things. Heart, liver and other organs can be eaten, either by people or in petfoods. Fat is partly sold with the lean meat, but much is processed for lard and margarine. Bones are boiled to make glue and the remains ground up for fertilizer and animal feed. Even the blood is useful – it makes a fine plant fertilizer.

▽ The stocky black cow below is an Aberdeen Angus, a typical beef breed. The sandy-colored dairy cow is a Jersey, which gives rich, creamy milk.

▷ These Holsteins are a very popular breed. Adults may weigh up to 1,320 lb (600 kg) and give up to ten times this weight in milk a year. The Jersey is a much smaller beast, weighing no more than 825 lb (375 kg).

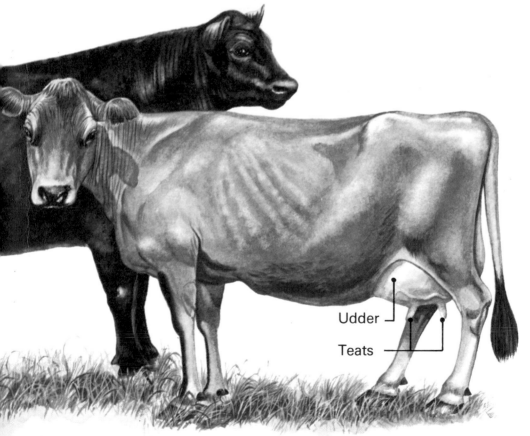

Udder

Teats

Calves and milking

△ Cows are very curious animals. This young female, a heifer, sniffed and tried to lick the photographer's camera a few moments after this picture was taken.

Cattle have a digestive system which enables them to eat grass and get nourishment from it. A cow changes her food into milk, which is very good for you. Grass is a cow's natural food, but the amount and quality of her milk is improved by adding other things to the diet. Farmers give their cows feeds like hay and cattle-cake, a mixture of ingredients such as barley, molasses and fish meal.

Cows are first mated when they are about two years old. They give birth some nine months later, when they produce their first milk. The calves are fed on milk substitutes while the cows give dairy milk for about ten months. From a maximum of perhaps 46 pints (22 liters) a day, a cow's milk yield gradually drops until her next calf is born. This yearly pattern carries on until the cow is too old to give birth or produce a good milk yield.

◁ Calves weigh up to 99 lb (45 kg) when they are born and can stand on wobbly legs within a couple of hours. When older, they play together in small groups.

▽ Suction cups are attached to the cows' teats in the milking parlor. A gentle mechanical action sucks the milk and pumps it to waiting containers.

Sheep

△ Sheepdogs are used all over the world to drive and gather sheep. A sheepdog can "freeze" a sheep just by staring at it.

Sheep were first bred and tamed some 7,000 years ago. There are now hundreds of breeds, each developed for a particular type of meat or wool.

Sheep are broadly divided into two groups, highland and lowland. Highland sheep have poor quality wool and give birth to fewer lambs, but can survive on cold and bare hillsides where lowland breeds would die.

The world's largest sheep producers are Australia and New Zealand. Merino sheep in Australia, originally from Spain, produce the finest quality wool in the world. In New Zealand, meat production is more important and frozen lamb has been exported for over a century. In 1851 New Zealand had 250,000 sheep. By 1974, the numbers had risen to 56 million.

Wherever sheep are raised, two jobs remain the shepherd's biggest tasks in a year – lambing and shearing.

▷ Hill sheep eat grass, heather and other small plants. The flock stays in one area, moving between favorite grazing spots and drinking from ponds and streams.

▽ These lowland sheep are grazing in rolling grassland just suited for them. Sheep have no front teeth on their upper jaws and crop grass by tearing at it.

Lambing and shearing

△ This picture shows sheep-shearers at work in Australia. They use electric clippers to remove the valuable woolly coat.

Springtime is lambing time. The rams and ewes were mated in the autumn before, and now, five months later, the ewes are ready to give birth to this year's lambs.

The newborn lambs stay close to their mother for the first few days, but soon get frisky and play with other lambs. Those raised for meat are sold before too long, the most tender lamb being about three months old.

Shearing is the next big job after lambing. As the spring turns into summer, a sheep will naturally shed its fleece in untidy lumps. The shearers clip off the fleece in one piece before this happens.

Like other farm animals, sheep have to be kept free of disease. A dose of medicine called drench keeps their stomach and lungs healthy. A dip into a disinfectant bath or spray kills off the parasites which live in the fleece.

14

△ Lowland lambs are usually born in twos, but triplets like this are not uncommon. They usually mean extra work for the farmer, as most ewes only have enough milk to feed two lambs properly.

◁ Lambs and their mothers recognize each other by their smell and call. The long and shaggy coat on this ewe will soon be ready for shearing.

Poultry

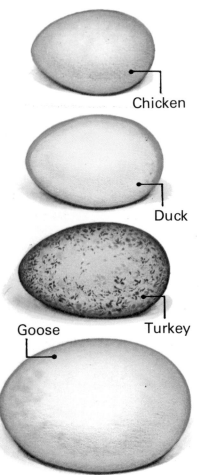

Chicken

Duck

Goose

Turkey

△ The eggs laid by different birds vary in size and shape. These four are shown about half life-size.

Poultry is the name given to all the different birds raised by farmers. They include chickens, turkeys, ducks and geese. By far the most important are chickens, which give meat and eggs.

Chickens raised for meat are kept in huge chicken houses, with up to 20,000 birds under one roof. Their food is carefully controlled to make them grow quickly. Diets vary, but the birds may be fed a nourishing mixture of corn, soybean and marigold petals, with vitamins and drugs to prevent disease. The birds do not live long – within two months they are big enough for the supermarket shelves.

Egg-laying birds are kept in a deep-litter house or battery cage. Both are types of large chicken houses where the food and light are controlled to encourage the birds to lay eggs. A hen lays about 275 eggs in its first year, about 17 times its body weight.

△ Chickens pecking about in the open like this are becoming a rare sight. They need more care and lay fewer eggs than birds kept in deep litter or battery cages. Free-range birds can also be attacked by foxes.

◁ The birds in this battery house live in wire cages. They eat and drink from troughs and their eggs roll from under their cages into collecting trays.

Turkeys, geese and ducks

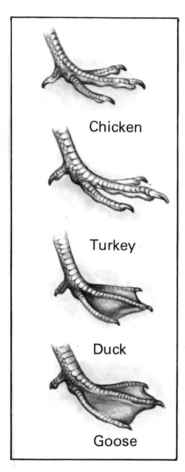

Chicken

Turkey

Duck

Goose

△ These pictures show the differences between the feet of land and water birds. The water birds have webbed feet, just right for swimming.

The turkey is a North American bird, brought to Europe in the sixteenth century. In Britain and North America it is traditional fare at Christmas, and also on Thanksgiving Day in the USA.

Like chicken farming, turkey rearing is big business. The birds are kept together in large numbers, usually in big wire enclosures. They need looking after quite carefully, as they can pick up diseases easily. Turkeys used to be huge birds, but today's breeds are smaller so they can easily fit into modern ovens.

Ducks and geese give both eggs and meat, though few people eat their eggs any more. Neither bird has as much flesh as a chicken or turkey. Duck down, the bird's fluffy feathers, is very soft and still fills the most expensive pillows. Goose feathers have been used to stuff pillows, for arrow feathers and as quill pens.

◁ Turkeys are kept in large enclosures. Smaller white breeds are replacing these huge creatures.

▽ Ducks and geese are both water birds and like to have a pond to splash about in. Because geese honk and hiss loudly if they are disturbed, they make very good "watchdogs."

Pigs

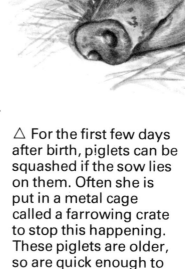

Pigs provide pork, bacon and ham. Those used for meat are usually kept indoors, where the comfortable conditions help them put on weight quickly. Those used for breeding usually live out in the open.

Pigs are cleaner in their habits than most farm animals, but they like to roll about in the mud when the weather is warm. This is not because they like dirt, but because they cannot sweat. So they try to cover themselves with a nice cool coating of mud or water. If the ground is dry, a pig will root out a shallow trench and lie down against the cool soil under the surface.

Female pigs, called sows, have lots of piglets. They can have two or three litters a year, each one with nine or more piglets. The world piglet record is held by a Danish sow which gave birth to a litter of no less than 34 in June 1961!

△ For the first few days after birth, piglets can be squashed if the sow lies on them. Often she is put in a metal cage called a farrowing crate to stop this happening. These piglets are older, so are quick enough to get out of the way.

▷ This Saddleback pig is enjoying a nice cool mud bath. It is a very warm day!

20

Goats

△ This is a Saanen goat which is cream or white. Other Swiss breeds are the brown Toggenberg and the Alpine, which can be white, brown, gray or black.

Goats are popular in hot countries where the grazing is too poor for sheep and cattle. They are found especially in the lands of the southern Mediterranean, the Middle East, Africa, South America and Asia.

Some breeds, such as the Angora, have fine silky hair. This is widely used as mohair for sweaters.

Special milking breeds were originally developed in Switzerland and in many countries people keep one or two goats just for the milk. It is of good quality, but even a good milker gives less than $6\frac{1}{4}$ pints (3 liters) a day.

Goats are agile climbers and browse on lots of different plants including thistles and other weeds. Unless stopped, they will also eat the bark of trees and even hedges. So they have to be tied up firmly or kept behind high fences.

△ This goat has a strong chain to keep her away from trees and hedges. Goats are very agile and some can even climb trees to nibble at the tasty young leaves at the branch tips.

▷ Goats are very nimble creatures. They can easily trot about the ledges, rocks and slopes of mountain areas.

Horses

Until tractors and other powered machines were developed, horses of various breeds were used on farms in many countries across the world.

Large, heavy draft horses, such as English Clydesdales and French Percherons, were used for jobs like plowing and pulling heavily laden hay carts. In North America the grasslands were harvested by reaper-binders pulled by big teams of up to 24 horses.

Rounding up cattle in the Wild West of the nineteenth century was a job for the horse-riding cowboy. Riding stock horses, cowboys drove cattle to freight yards to be sold. The other job was the round-up. The cattle, which had lived almost wild on the range, were found and counted.

Today there are few horses doing hauling work. They are still used on large farms for rounding up sheep and cattle.

△ Draft horses are those used for plowing and heavy hauling work. Plowing like this is now rarely done except in show competitions. Tractors have taken over the job.

▷ Sundown on the range. Sheep farmers in Australia and New Zealand also use the horse as a basic means of getting about.

Farm animal breeds

On these pages you can see just a few of the hundreds of breeds of sheep and cattle. Some are best for their meat or wool, others for their meat or milk.

◁ **Scottish Blackface.** Very good meat and long wool, which is used to make carpets and tweed, a type of clothing material.

▽ **Border Leicester.** An English breed, with long fleece and good quality meat.

△ **Merino.** Famous for the fine quality of its wool. Originally bred in Spain, now important in Australia.

▷ **Oxford Down.** Large, meaty quality wool breed.

◁ **North American Holstein**. A dairy cow which gives a good supply of milk. It is bulkier than the European Friesian.

▷ **Guernsey**. A dairy cow, one of the smaller breeds of cattle. Gives rich, creamy milk.

◁ **Charolais**. A French beef breed. A full-grown bull like this may weigh up to 1.65 tons.

▷ **Hereford**. A common beef breed in the USA, Britain, Canada, South America and Australia.

More farm animal breeds

Farmers develop new varieties of animal by mating males and females of different breeds. They might wish, for example, to combine the meaty body of one pure-breed with the quiet nature of another breed. Animals with parents of different breeds are called cross-breeds or hybrids. All farm animals have been improved over the years using such breeding methods.

◁ **Saddleback**. Named after the broad, pale band over its shoulders and front legs. Kept for bacon and pork, though the meat is fatty.

▽ **Duroc**. A fast-growing pork breed, very popular in the USA.

△ **Gloucester Old Spot**. One of the oldest pure-breeds. Many new breeds have been developed from it.

▷ **Landrace**. Different types of Landrace are found throughout Europe.

28

△ **Rhode Island Red**. Many egg-laying hybrids have been bred from this bird.

△ **White Leghorn**. Another popular pure-breed for egg-laying hybrids.

△ **Light Sussex**. Heavy and quiet bird, reared for its meat as well as eggs.

▽ A mule is a cross between a horse and a donkey. It cannot reproduce. Donkeys, like mules, carry people and their loads in many countries

Mule

Donkey

△ **Clydesdale**. A draft horse, used for hauling work. Spot the "feathers" of fine hair round its lower legs.

Farm animal facts

Here are some interesting facts about the world of farm animals.

The aurochs, ancestor of cattle breeds, was a huge beast. A full-grown bull was 6.5 ft (2 m) high at the shoulders. The last aurochs died in Poland in 1627.

Roast goose was the favorite meal of Queen Elizabeth I of England. It was served on Michaelmas Day, 29 September.

The American Duroc pig is descended from those brought over by Christopher Columbus in the 15th century.

A new breed in the USA is the Beefalo. It is a mixture of Hereford, Charolais and buffalo, the animal which used to roam the plains in huge herds.

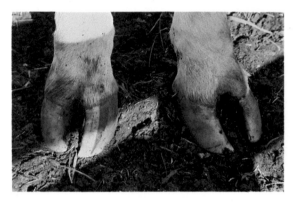

△ Cattle are cloven-hoofed animals. The picture and hoofprint above show the two toes on each hoof. Other cloven-hoofed farm animals are sheep, pigs and goats.

Altogether in 1981, American farmers produced 3,881,000,000 chickens. This is more than 17 for each man, woman and child in the country.

The biggest hen's egg ever was laid by an American Leghorn chicken. The monster egg weighed in at a staggering 16 oz (454 grams)! In 1981 hens in the USA laid nearly 70 billion eggs.

Pigs can be useful other than for pork and bacon. In France they are used to sniff out truffles, a type of underground mushroom used for dishes in expensive restaurants. Dogs can also do the job, but pigs are much better. One snag is that they like the truffles, so the keepers have to make sure the pigs do not gobble up the truffles as soon as they find them.

30

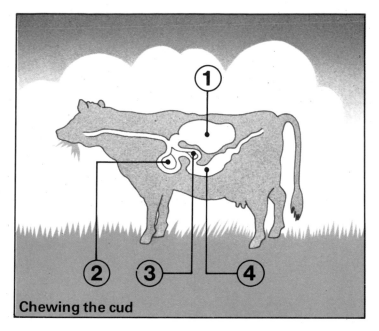
Chewing the cud

Here is a list of some of the technical words in this book.

Breed
One of the varieties of a particular animal. Jersey and Holstein are two breeds of cattle.

△ A cow can eat grass and get nourishment from it. The grass is swallowed without much chewing. It goes into the rumen (1). When a cow "chews the cud," she brings lumps of food back up into the mouth for a second, thorough chew. The food is then swallowed again and passes into the other stomachs, the reticulum (2) and omasum (3). Finally it passes into the abomasum (4). This is where the goodness in the food is taken into the bloodstream, as in human stomachs. Animals like cows, sheep and goats which chew the cud are called ruminants.

The top lip of a sheep is split. It moves apart when pressed against the ground, which allows the sheep to crop grass very closely. A sheep can eat grass which is far too short for cows or horses.

The record for sheep-shearing is 694 lambs, sheared in nine hours in 1975. Using a pair of hand-clippers, a New Zealand shearer managed 353 lambs in the same time in 1976.

Ewe
Adult female sheep. An adult male is a ram; a baby is a lamb.

Free range
Chickens which are allowed to grow up in the open air, rather than being kept in deep litter houses or battery cages.

Hybrid
Animal created by mating parents of different breeds, to get the best features of each.

Ruminant
An animal which chews the cud, such as a cow, sheep or goat.

31

Index